Sacramental Initiation

Complete in Baptism

by

E. C. Whitaker

Vicar of Plumpton Wall, Penrith
Honorary Canon of Carlisle
Member of the Church of England Liturgical Commission

GROVE BOOKS

BRAMCOTE   NOTTS.

CONTENTS

ACKNOWLEDGEMENT

The quotations on pages 27 and 28 from the Ancient Christian Writers Series, vol. 31, *St. John Chrysostom: Baptismal Instructions* (edited by P. W. Harkins) are reprinted by kind permission of the copyright holders, the Paulist Press, New York, U.S.A.

First Impresssion April 1975

ISSN 0306 0608
ISBN 0 901710 64 4

EDITORIAL FOREWORD

For well over three years the series of 'Grove Booklets on Ministry and Worship' has continued to appear every month (except for one month off in the Summer), and there has built up a world-wide clientele—many taking them on standing order. This provides a point from which a further step forward can be taken. The present monograph is therefore denominated 'Grove Liturgical Study No. 1', and it is not only slightly larger than the standard Booklet on Ministry and Worship, it is also less concerned to be popular. It is a piece of academic work, and heralds other similar titles, to be published quarterly in this new series.

It is a very happy event that Canon Charles Whitaker has been able to contribute the first of these 'Liturgical Studies'. He has made for himself a name as a fine scholar in the field of Christian initiation, and he is also a very hard-working and deeply respected member of the Church of England Liturgical Commission, where I have got to know him over a period of almost ten years. His writings are well-known, and are listed on the outside back cover. But what he insists about himself is that his interests are those of a parish priest, concerned about the pastoral use of liturgy, and the real problems of worship for the local church.

Thus, although this study is academic, it also proves to be relevant and timely. Charles Whitaker is no propagandist, and he reaches the conclusions contained in the title in a scholarly correct style. But in the context of the current debate on initiation in the Church of England, the conclusions affect not only the content of liturgical texts, but the whole pattern of initiation on which General Synod has to decide in 1976. The issue as to whether baptism in water *is* complete sacramental initiation was proposed to General Synod as the first and great issue to be decided when they first debated the matter in February 1974—that is how the working paper by P. R. Cornwell saw it. But the Standing Committee did not present it to Synod as an issue at all, and the matters which were referred to the dioceses did not clearly contain this question. So Charles Whitaker's study is a recall to basic principles.

Colin Buchanan

March 1975

1 THE PRACTICE OF CONFIRMATION IN THE WESTERN CHURCH

Among the written records of the western Church, the earliest account we have of the rites of Christian initiation is provided in a work written to defend Christianity against its detractors by Justin Martyr, who died about the year 165. There is no reason to suppose that he gives an exhaustive and complete account of everything which happened, but so far as his account takes us the rite of initiation seems to have been very simple. It consisted of the washing of the candidate in water 'in the name of the Father and Lord God of all things, and of our Saviour Jesus Christ, and of the Holy Spirit'. The whole initiation, so far as Justin describes it, was thus accomplished in the water of baptism with the invocation of the Holy Trinity.[1] Since Justin's day many accounts have been written of the rites of Christian initiation at different times and in different places. Some of them are descriptions of the rite in sermons and similar works, others are texts of the 'service' as it was performed, but none of them describes a rite as simple as Justin's. In every case the baptismal bath was followed by one or more other ceremonies, and our first business is to note what they were.

1. Tertullian was a priest in Africa and in the year 198 he wrote a treatise *Concerning Baptism.* He says 'we come up from the washing and are anointed with the blessed unction' and goes on to explain this anointing by reference to the Old Testament custom of anointing priests. Later he continues 'Next follows the imposition of the hand in benediction, inviting and welcoming the Holy Spirit'. So Tertullian indicates at least two ceremonies after baptism, first an anointing and then an imposition of the hand.[2]

2. The *Apostolic Tradition* of Hippolytus was written in Rome about the year 215 and describes a rather more complex set of ceremonies. After he has come up from the baptismal water and before he has dried himself and put on his clothes, the candidate is anointed, almost certainly by a priest, with the words 'I anoint thee with holy oil in the name of Jesus Christ'. He then appears before the bishop. A prayer is appointed for the bishop to say, and it is very probable that he said the prayer once over all the baptized as they stood together, with his hands extended towards them. Then the bishop 'pouring the consecrated oil and laying his hands on his head' says 'I anoint thee with holy oil in God the Father Almighty, and Christ Jesus, and the Holy Ghost'. The bishop then seals him on the forehead, that is to say he signs the cross on his forehead, and gives him the kiss of peace.[3]

3. St Ambrose gives us an account of the initiation rites in Milan at the close of the fourth century in his addresses to the newly baptized.[4] When the candidate came up from the water, he was first anointed on the head by the bishop, with the words 'God the Father Almighty, who

1 *Documents of the Baptismal Liturgy,* ed. E. C. Whitaker, p.2. (This work is cited below as DBL, and references are to the second, 1970 edition).

2 DBL p.8.

3 DBL p.6.

4 DBL p.p.130-133.

hath regenerated thee with water and the Holy Ghost, and hath forgiven thee thy sins, himself anoint thee unto eternal life'. There followed a ceremony known as the pedilavium, or washing of the candidates' feet, and then the vesting in white robes. Last of all there was the 'spiritual seal' which St. Ambrose also calls the 'perfecting', when 'the Holy Spirit is bestowed, the spirit of wisdom and understanding, the spirit of counsel and strength, the spirit of knowledge and godliness, the spirit of holy fear, as it were, the seven virtues of the Holy Spirit'. Exactly what actions were involved in the spiritual seal is not at all clear from St. Ambrose's description. It almost certainly included a signing with the cross and very possibly either an anointing with oil or the laying on of hands, or both.[1] We may note that the passage which we have just quoted from St. Ambrose is the earliest known reference to a prayer which survives to this day both in the Prayer Book and in the Roman Catholic ritual. That is the prayer for the sevenfold gifts of the Holy Spirit which were associated with the Messiah (see Is. 11.2 and Luke 4.18). This prayer has a long history in the Church and we shall refer to it in future as the Confirmation Prayer.

4. The practice of the church in Rome from a date at least as early as the beginning of the sixth century is known to us from the Gelasian Sacramentary.[2] After the baptismal washing the candidate was first signed on the head with chrism by a priest (chrism is oil made fragrant with perfume). The bishop then says the Confirmation Prayer, and the text in the Gelasian Sacramentary runs as follows:

> Almighty God, Father of our Lord Jesus Christ, who hast made thy servants to be regenerated of water and the Holy Spirit, and hast given them remission of all their sins, do thou Lord send upon them thy Holy Spirit the Paraclete, and give them the spirit of wisdom and understanding, the spirit of counsel and might, the spirit of knowledge and godliness, and fill them with the spirit of the fear of God, in the name of our Lord Jesus Christ with whom thou livest and reignest ever God with the Holy Spirit, throughout all ages of ages. Amen.

The rubric says that the bishop is to 'lay his hand on them' as he says this prayer, and this most probably means that he extended his hands over all the newly baptized while he said the prayer once. After that he signed each one on the forehead with chrism, saying 'The sign of Christ unto life eternal'.

5. The *Missale Gothicum*[3] provides a good example of the kind of thing which happened in the Gallican Church about the year 700 and we cannot say for how long before that. Everything was performed by a priest. After the baptism the priest was to 'touch him with chrism' ('pour chrism over his brow': Bobbio Missal)[4] saying 'I anoint thee with the chrism of holiness, the garment of immortality,

---

[1] See J. D. C. Fisher, *Christian Initiation: Baptism in the Medieval West*, Alcuin Club, 1965, for a full discussion of this and other texts.
[2] DBL p.188.
[3] DBL p.162.
[4] DBL p.212.

which our Lord Jesus Christ first received from the Father, that thou mayest bear it entire and spotless before the judgment seat of Christ, and live unto all eternity'. There followed the washing of the feet, the vesting in a white robe, and that was all.

Our survey is not quite complete, but we must pause here to notice one thing in particular which it has revealed. In some parts of the western Church, certainly in Rome but less certainly in other places, some of the ceremonies after baptism were reserved strictly to the bishop. In the Gelasian Sacramentary, for instance, this applied to the Confirmation Prayer, to the extension of the bishop's hands which accompanied it, and to the anointing which followed it. This led to an important development in the rites of initiation. With the growth and expansion of the Church, bishops could not always be present at every baptism, especially when they were performed in emergency. The consequence was that those rites which were the prerogative of the bishop had to be deferred until the candidate could be presented to the bishop. This is the only reason why confirmation came to be separated from baptism. In normal circumstances, when the bishop was present, all candidates were baptized and anointed and received the laying on of hands, and this applied to adults and infants alike. If it seemed proper to the early Church to baptize infants, then it seemed proper also to perform over them all those other ceremonies which were associated with baptism. Infant confirmation was thus the normal practice. The notion that baptism was appropriate to infants but that the ceremonies after baptism were appropriate only to Christians of mature years would have surprised the Church in the early centuries and only developed in the middle ages. However the separation of baptism from the ceremonies which followed it was the inevitable consequence of the expansion of the Church and the reservation of the post-baptismal ceremonies to the bishops. Thus long before the Reformation the custom was established that normally, though not invariably, the rite called confirmation was deferred until children were seven years old or more.

6. Such is the situation represented in the books of the Sarum rite up to the eve of the Reformation.[1] Baptism was administered in infancy: some years later at confirmation the bishop recited the Confirmation Prayer, and then, anointing his thumb with chrism, he marked the child with chrism in the form of a cross on his brow, saying 'I sign thee, N., with the sign of the cross, and I confirm thee with the chrism of salvation, in the name of the Father and of the Son and of the Holy Spirit'. There is no reference in the Sarum rite to the laying on of hands or the extension of hands, although this was included in books of the Roman rite of the period.

7. Our survey ends with the familiar service in the Book of Common Prayer. The reformers regarded the rite of anointing as unscriptural and therefore replaced it with the laying on of hands, after the example of the apostles who had laid hands on the Samaritan converts and on others in Ephesus (Acts 8.17 and 19.6). They preserved the ancient Confirmation Prayer, but with significant differences which we shall note later: and they provided a new form of words to accompany the laying on of hands.

[1] J. D. C. Fisher, *op. cit.* p.p.180-5.

2 THE GIFT OF THE HOLY SPIRIT

We have traced the confirmation service as we know it today from a date at the very end of the second century. We have taken note of the outward signs which were employed in the post-baptismal ceremonies from the time of Tertullian. Some of them we can disregard, such as the *pedilavium* and the vesting with white robes, for they are obviously irrelevant to our inquiry. We are left with the fact that after baptism the newly baptized went on to be anointed or to receive the laying on of hands, or both. We have noted not only the variety of external signs but also the variety of formularies which accompanied them: and it is clear that there existed no one form or pattern of words about which it can be said they are the form or pattern of words which ought to be used. Our next task is to observe the meanings which the Church has assigned to these rites and the inter-pretations which have been placed on them. Of course the meaning which we attach to confirmation will depend in some degree on the meaning which we attach to baptism, since the two are evidently related to each other in some way: and many interpretations of the rite are related to the fact that the Christian is described in the New Testament as one who has received the gift of the Holy Spirit. It will therefore be useful, before we examine the meanings of confirmation, to look at some passages in the New Testament in order to explain what we mean by the 'gift of the Spirit'.

The New Testament describes to us the dawning of the Messianic age, in which the prophecies and expectations of the Old Testament were being fulfilled: and an important part of this expectation was the outpouring of the Holy Spirit. Thus when Jesus returned in the power of the Spirit to Galilee and preached in the synagogue at Nazareth, he explained himself and his mission as the fulfilment of Isaiah's prophecy about the Messiah. He said 'The Spirit of the Lord is upon me, because he has anointed me to preach good news to the poor' (Luke 4.18, quoting Is. 61.1). Similarly, when the Holy Spirit took possession of the apostles at Pentecost and sent them out into the streets to preach the gospel, St. Peter explained their action by claiming that the words of the prophet Joel were being fulfilled 'In the last days, it shall be, God declares, that I will pour out my Spirit on all flesh' (Acts 2.17, quoting Joel 2.28). In the same speech Peter promised that this outpouring of the Spirit would be extended to others. He said 'Repent and be baptized . . . and you shall receive the gift of the Spirit' (Acts 2.38). The possession of the Spirit was a characteristic mark of the men of the new age, so that later St. Paul could say 'If a man does not possess the Spirit of Christ, he is no Christian' (Rom. 8.19). St. Paul speaks of the Christian community as the place where the Spirit dwells, for writing to the Christians in Corinth he says 'Surely you know that you are God's temple, where the Spirit of God dwells?' (1 Cor. 3.16): and later in the same epistle he says that the same is true of the individual Christian: 'Do you not know that your body is a shrine of the indwelling Holy Spirit, the Spirit is God's gift to you?' (1 Cor. 6.19). This gift had already been promised by Jesus to the apostles and we may suppose to all his disciples, when he said 'I will pray the Father and he will give you another Counsellor, to be with you for ever, even the Spirit of truth . . . you know him, for he dwells with you and shall be in you' (John 14.16, 17).

St. Paul speaks of the Holy Spirit 'dwelling in us' and so does our Lord in the gospel. Of course this is picture language to describe what is past description. The language of Acts is different, but it intends to describe the same reality. One brief passage includes three different pictures, for in the tenth chapter (verses 44-48) we read of the Holy Spirit 'falling on all who heard the word', of the gift of the Spirit being 'poured out', and of people who had 'received the Spirit'. All these different kinds of expression are designed to express the same reality which St. Paul described when he spoke of the Holy Spirit 'dwelling' in the Christian: and that is the reality with which we are concerned in our consideration of baptism and confirmation.

The natural consequence of receiving the Spirit or experiencing the outpouring of the Spirit is that Christians display in their character and conduct some of the graces and virtues which arise because of his presence within them. Thus St. Paul traces to the presence of the one Spirit within the Church a variety of gifts such as wisdom, faith, prophecy, etc (1 Cor. 12.4-11). Similarly, from the presence of the Spirit we should reap a harvest of love, joy, peace, and other virtues (Gal. 5.22). But the consequences of possessing the Spirit are not the same thing as the actual possession, and it is therefore necessary to recognise a clear distinction between the *gift* of the Spirit on the one hand, that is to say the presence of the Holy Spirit dwelling in us, and the *gifts* of the Holy Spirit, on the other hand, that is to say the gifts and virtues which result from his indwelling.

In many passages of the New Testament we find that the early Church associated the gift of the indwelling Spirit with the rites of initiation. Thus, to quote but two examples, St. Peter said to the crowds at Pentecost 'Repent and be baptized . . . and you will receive the gift of the Holy Spirit' (Acts 2.38): and similarly St. Paul said 'God saved us through the water of rebirth and the renewing power of the Holy Spirit' (Titus 3.5). Less usual was the occasion when the Holy Spirit fell on Cornelius and his household as soon as they had heard St. Peter's proclamation of the gospel and before they were baptized: but even in that case the descent of the Spirit on Cornelius and the rest was regarded as a reason for proceeding to baptism without delay. These texts and others like them make it plain that from the beginning the Church associated the gift of the Spirit with the occasion when men entered the Church in the rites of initiation: but whether this gift was conveyed specifically in the baptism in water, or whether possibly it was conveyed in some other rites after baptism, is a matter to which we must now turn.

3 INTERPRETATIONS

In 1890, in a book called *The Relation of Confirmation to Baptism,*[1] Dr. A. J. Mason expounded the view that baptism in water and the laying on of hands are two signs which make up one sacrament. He compared this sacrament of initiation with Holy Communion,[2] in which one sacrament exists in the two signs of bread and wine. In the one sacrament of initiation, Mason claimed that in the water of baptism the Holy Spirit operates as it were from outside the candidate to convey the gifts of new birth and remission of sins, but that the gift of the indwelling Spirit was bestowed only in the laying on of hands, or in the anointing which was accepted as a substitute for it. He thus regarded the first sign and its effects as a mere preparation for the second sign which conveyed the Holy Spirit. Mason had no difficulty in assembling a large number of texts from the Fathers and the liturgies of the western Church which seemed to prove his point, and it will be convenient here to notice a few examples of them. In Tertullian's treatise *Concerning Baptism,* to which we have already referred, Tertullian says 'Not that we obtain the Holy Spirit in the water, but having been cleansed in the water we are prepared for the Holy Spirit': and later he says 'Next follows the imposition of the hand in benediction, inviting and welcoming the Holy Spirit'.[3] On the face of it these two passages taken together seem to leave no doubt that in Tertullian's mind it was the laying on of hands which he associated with the gift of the Spirit, for which the baptism in water was a mere preparation. Cyprian of Carthage[4] a generation later seemed to teach the same thing. He said 'Moreover a man is not born again through the imposition of the hand, when he receives the Holy Spirit, but in baptism, so as to be born first and receive the Spirit after, as was the case with the first man Adam. God formed him first, and then breathed into his nostrils the breath of life. For the Spirit cannot be received without the man first being in existence to receive him'. Not all passages which Mason quotes are as clear as these two, and even when they are it would be a mistake to assume that they represent fully the beliefs of their authors: their impact may need to be modified by other passages, even from the same writer. For instance when Tertullian says 'not that we obtain the Holy Spirit in the water' we wonder why he should go out of his way to make this disclaimer if he was not conscious of a belief that the Spirit *is* conveyed in the water.[5] Nevertheless the view that the Holy Spirit was given in the post-baptismal ceremonies was widespread in the western Church and had the support of powerful authority. Thus in a letter of advice to a provincial bishop Pope Innocent wrote the following: 'The right of bishops alone to seal and to deliver the Spirit the Paraclete is proved not only by the custom of the Church but also by that reading in the Acts of the Apostles which tells how Peter and John were directed to deliver the Holy Spirit to people who were already baptized. For it is permissible for presbyters . . . to anoint with chrism, but only with such as has been

---

[1] London, second edition, 1893.
[2] Mason, *op. cit.* p.2.
[3] Mason, *op. cit.* pp.59f.
[4] Mason, *op. cit.* pp.64f.
[5] See G. W. H. Lampe, *The Seal of the Spirit,* London, 1951, pp.157f.

consecrated by the bishop: and even then they are not to sign the brow with that oil, for that is reserved to bishops alone when they deliver the Spirit the Paraclete'.[1] There can be no doubt that the repeated mention of 'the Spirit the Paraclete' are echoes of the Confirmation Prayer, and the rubric which preceded that prayer in the Gelasian Sacramentary ran 'Then the sevenfold Spirit is given by the bishop. To seal them he lays his hand upon them with these words . . .'.[2]

It was evidence of this kind which encouraged Mason to believe that the gift of the Holy Spirit in Christian initation is bestowed in the ceremonies which follow baptism and that baptism itself is only a preparation for confirmation. Whether he interpreted his evidence correctly, and whether he examined it fully, are matters which need not concern us here, except to note that Dr. G. W. H. Lampe in *The Seal of the Spirit* has shown reason to doubt it. Our immediate concern is to note the conclusions which Mason drew from his study of the evidence. He says that 'if we are to be guided by primitive antiquity, confirmation is an integral part of baptism, in such a way that what we normally call baptism is, without it, an unfinished fragment'. He goes on to add that 'notwithstanding any previous operation of the Holy Ghost upon the soul, the baptized but unconfirmed believer may, unless the divine action departs from its normal course, be truly said not to have received the Holy Ghost'.[3]

The time came when in the more settled parts of Europe the vast majority of people were baptized in infancy and confirmed, if they were confirmed at all, when they reached adolescence or adult years. Accordingly a new approach developed which taught that baptism is the sacrament appropriate to infancy, conveying new life and such gifts as the infant needs, and that confirmation is the sacrament appropriate to maturity. The Christian was compared to a soldier who must first be enlisted and later supplied with arms. Baptism was compared to the soldier's enlistment, confirmation armed him for Christian warfare and gave him strength to confess his faith before men. This understanding of confirmation was succinctly expressed in the twelfth century by Peter Lombard, who said that the *virtus sacramenti* in confirmation is the imparting of the Holy Spirit for vigorous action, whereas the Spirit is given in baptism for the remission of sins.[4] The same teaching received its classic expression in the *Summa* of St. Thomas Aquinas, whose authority has ensured it a wide acceptance in the doctrine of the Roman Catholic Church up to the present day. He said 'It has already been said that as baptism is a kind of regeneration into the Christian life, so also confirmation is a kind of spiritual growth, advancing the man into perfect spiritual age. Now it is manifest from the analogy of the bodily life that the action of a human being newly born is one thing, and the action which belongs to him on arriving at perfect age is another. And therefore by the sacrament of confirmation is given to the man the spiritual power to do certain sacred actions over and above those which he was empowered to do in baptism. For in baptism the man receives power to do those things

---

[1] DBL p.229.
[2] DBL p.188.
[3] Mason, *op. cit.* p.414.
[4] Fisher, *op. cit.* p.128

which pertain to his own salvation, as living a life of his own; but in confirmation the man receives power to do those things which pertain to the spiritual combat against the foes of the faith; as appears from the example of the apostles, who before they received the fulness of the Holy Ghost were in the upper chamber, continuing in prayer, but afterwards went forth and were not afraid publicly to confess their faith, even before the enemies of the Christian faith'.[1]

Mason objected to this doctrine that a sacrament given once and for all does not fulfil the natural requirements of a 'sacrament of growth', which would need to be given from time to time during the season of growth. He claims that 'the Holy Eucharist is the sacrament which answers to the nutriment by which the spiritual life is sustained'.[2] However this may be, the thomistic doctrine has one serious weakness in its assumption that confirmation is necessarily administered to people in mature years. In the middle ages, during which this doctrine developed, that was indeed the case, but we have seen that from the beginning of the third century the laying on of hands and anointing were normally administered to infants no less than adults, and we would therefore be justified in supposing that any satisfactory doctrine of confirmation must be consistent with the idea of infant confirmation. The teaching of the middle ages was not consistent with infant confirmation, and this was its fatal flaw.[3]

The reformers of the sixteenth century based their understanding of confirmation on their interpretation of the incidents described in the Acts of the Apostles when the apostles laid hands on the Samaritan converts, and on others at Ephesus. From the time of Cyprian in the middle of the third century these narratives had been widely accepted as the prime scriptural examples of confirmation. But many of the reformers regarded the incidents which they relate as isolated events which St. Luke recorded for their historical interest, and denied that they were to be taken as typical or as examples to be followed by the Church.[4] The logic of their argument justified them in abandoning the practice of confirmation, and some did. Others accepted the laying on of hands as a solemn but not strictly necessary observance, which deserved to be maintained because it had been practised by the apostles. All the reformers were however biassed against confirmation, because in their experience the Church administered it with chrism only, for which they found no warrant in scripture. Their tendency therefore was to regard baptism as the occasion for the gift of the Spirit and to regard the laying on of hands as no more than a solemn blessing; to deny that it was a sacrament instituted by our Lord; but to accept it as a suitable occasion of prayer for the gifts of the Spirit. Like St. Thomas, they knew of confirmation only in connection with adolescents or adults, and so regarded it as a suitable occasion for people who had reached years of discretion and were capable of answering for their faith. Archbishop Cranmer believed that 'there is no place in scripture that

1 Mason, *op. cit.* p.47. See also Fisher, *op. cit.* p.129.
2 Mason, *op. cit.* pp.420f.
3 Fisher, *op. cit.* pp.134f.
4 For the views of the reformers, see J. D. C. Fisher, *Christian Initiation: The Reformation Period*, Alcuin Club, 1970, pp.159-260.

declareth this sacrament to be instituted of Christ, for the places alleged for the same be no institutions but acts and deeds of the apostles', and consistently with this he concluded that 'the efficacy of this sacrament is of such value as is the prayer of the bishop made in the name of the Church'.[1]

The Book of Common Prayer and the Thirty-Nine Articles were products of the Reformation and the teaching of the reformers shines through them. The 25th of the Articles thus makes a distinction between baptism and confirmation in that baptism is 'ordained of Christ' whereas confirmation, in common with other rites commonly called sacraments, had not any 'visible sign or ceremony ordained of God'. This distinction seems to imply that baptism must be an essential part of Christian initiation, since it is ordained of Christ, but that confirmation is not essential since it is not so ordained. A rubric in the Prayer Book provides that no-one may be admitted to Holy Communion until he has been confirmed or wishes to be confirmed: but the purpose of this may be no more than to impose a discipline, which is a long way from saying that confirmation is essential to initiation, or an essential preliminary to communion. In the confirmation service itself there is nothing to indicate that this is an occasion when the Holy Spirit comes to the candidate for the first time, to take up his dwelling in the candidate. The ancient Confirmation Prayer is indeed preserved in the service, but with the significant and deliberate difference that whereas the old prayer had said 'Send upon them the sevenfold Holy Ghost, the Paraclete, from heaven', the new prayer says 'Strengthen them with the Holy Ghost the Comforter, and daily increase in them thy manifold gifts of grace'. Similarly, the new formulary which accompanies the laying on of hands includes the prayer 'that they may daily increase in thy Holy Spirit more and more'. There is nothing in the Prayer Book revision of these prayers to suggest that the gift of the indwelling Spirit is to be bestowed on candidates who have not yet received the gift, or that the laying on of the bishop's hands was expected to convey such a gift. In the prayer which follows the laying on of hands, the practice is justified only on the ground that it accords with the example of the apostles.

The catechism states that in baptism we are made 'members of Christ', and we may think it difficult to imagine a member of Christ who is not at the same time a 'temple of the Holy Ghost', or a Christian who belongs to the Body of Christ and does not at the same time possess his Spirit. The implication of these words in the Catechism seems therefore to be that the Spirit is given us in baptism. The baptism service itself includes such passages as 'Sanctify him with the Holy Ghost', and 'that all things belonging to the Spirit may live and grow in him'. There is also the prayer 'Give thy Holy Spirit that he may be born again'. It has been claimed that this prayer limits the work performed by the Holy Spirit in baptism to effecting new birth.[2] However the teaching of the Church of England is declared in the service for adult baptism no less than in the service for infant baptism, and in that service we find this plain and unqualified statement: 'Doubt ye not therefore, but earnestly believe that he [God] will bestow upon him the Holy Ghost'.

---

1 Fisher, *The Reformation Period*, pp.210, 219.
2 Mason, *op. cit.* p.427.

The Church of England at the Reformation, in common with other reforming bodies, attached a profession of faith or a renewal of baptismal vows to the laying on of hands, and thus ensured that the medieval notion of confirmation as an observance appropriate to growth should be preserved in the Anglican tradition. Although there is not a shred of evidence to support it, some of the reformers seriously believed that the practice of presenting adolescents to the bishop to renew their baptismal vows was followed in the primitive Church.[1] This belief is reiterated by Bishop Cosin in the introduction which he drew up for a new order of confirmation. In the same document he commended confirmation, and claimed that 'our warrant for the good effect thereof is the same which Patriarchs, the Prophets, the Apostles, and men of God have practised and found before us'. He upheld the view that confirmation is not of dominical institution and called it 'a sacred and solemn action of religion'. The Anglican tradition is well summed up in the following passage from Hamon L'Estrange's *Alliance of Divine Offices.* He says 'But that it is so [i.e. a sacrament] in true propriety of speech our adversaries shall never obtain from us, until they can find *verbum et elementum,* and both of Christ's institution, to meet in it; neither of which, as they confess, are yet to be found, their great Cardinal [i.e. Bellarmine] putting us off for both to "tradition unwritten". But although we entertain it not as a sacrament, yet being of apostolical practice . . . we . . . have not yet so slight a value for it as absolutely to reject it, being well persuaded that, accompanied with such fervent prayers, it will be the readier way to convey those graces of the Holy Spirit into the soul of the party baptized, which are necessary to "establish him in every good word and work". For the gift of the Holy Ghost, in order to which this rite is used, is not so much an effect of the hands imposed as of the invocation then applied: *ad invocationem sacerdotis Spiritus Sanctus infunditur,* saith St. Ambrose very well. "At the invocation of the bishop the Holy Ghost is infused."[2] Cosin and L'Estrange were faithful to the teaching of the Articles and of the Prayer Book, and represent the main stream of Anglican tradition in the matter. Bishop Sparrow in his *Rationale upon the Book of Common Prayer* goes no further, though he reads very much as though he would like to. But Charles Wheatly, writing in 1710, was one who did not hesitate to claim that we owe confirmation 'to a much more divine original, even to the example and institution of our blessed Lord'. He justifies this statement, quite at variance with Anglican teaching, by reference to the descent of the Spirit on our Lord at his baptism and his promises that he would send the Spirit to the apostles (Matt. 3.11; Acts 1.4). Wheatly's *Rational Illustration of the Book of Common Prayer* became a standard work until the middle of the nineteenth century and may well have influenced Mason. But although Wheatly varied from most of his contemporaries in his views about the origin of confirmation, he followed the familiar pattern of belief that baptism and confirmation are for infancy and growth respectively and repeated the medieval teaching that 'when we are baptized we are only listed under the banner of Christ: and not till confirmation equipped for battle'.

[1] Fisher, *The Reformation Period,* pp.171, 175, 182f, 194, 258.

[2] Quotations from Cosin, L'Estrange, and others are conveniently collected in *Anglicanism,* ed. P. E. More and F. L. Cross, London, 1957, pp.443-453.

The twentieth century has seen a succession of official Anglican reports on the theology and practice of confirmation, and other studies relating to it. It will be convenient to list the more important, as follows:

1912   Darwell Stone: *Holy Baptism*
1928   The Book of Common Prayer Revised (1928)
1936   Dom G. Dix: *Confirmation, or the Laying on of Hands* (Theology Occasional Papers, 5)
1938   Report: *Doctrine in the Church of England.* (Archbishops' Commission)
1944   Report: *Confirmation Today.* (Convocation Committees)
1946   Dom G. Dix: *The Theology of Confirmation in Relation to Baptism.*
1947   A. E. J. Rawlinson, Bishop of Derby: *Christian Initiation.*
1948   Report: *The Theology of Christian Initiation.* (Archbishops' Commission).
1948   Report of Lambeth Conference.
1949   Report: *Baptism Today.* (Convocation Committees)
1951   Dr. G. W. H. Lampe: *The Seal of the Spirit.*
1954   L. S. Thornton, C. R. *Confirmation, Its place in the Baptismal Mystery.*
1955   Report: *Baptism and Confirmation Today.* (Convocation Committees, including a minority report)
1958   Report of Lambeth Conference.
1967   M. Perry, ed. *Crisis for Confirmation.* See especially article by Canon J. D. C. Fisher.
1968   Report of Lambeth Conference.
1971   Report: *Christian Initiation: Birth and Growth in the Christian Society.* (Archbishops' Commission on Christian Initiation)

The reader may not be surprised to learn that the three main approaches to confirmation which we have noted on earlier pages all reappear in one or other of the official reports which are listed above. Thus the minority report in *Baptism and Confirmation Today* does not say in so many words, as Mason did, that baptism without confirmation is an unfinished fragment, or that the baptized but unconfirmed person cannot be said to have received the Holy Spirit, but that is undoubtedly what its authors meant, and the report amounts to a useful precis of Mason's thesis, amended and brought up to date in some respects.

The medieval doctrine that confirmation is the sacrament of growth was based not only on the assumption that it is administered to people in their maturity but also on the belief that it was divinely instituted. There was however a latent inconsistency in the teaching of Darwell Stone, who followed the Articles in denying dominical institution to confirmation but nevertheless tacitly treated its origin in the apostolic practice (as he supposed) as the equivalent of dominical institution, and therefore invested with sacramental efficacy. Stone[1] claims the evidence of the Prayer Book to show that 'the Church of England is committed with some definiteness to the belief that the gift of the Holy Spirit in baptism is of a very real kind, and has used such language which it would be difficult to

---

[1] D. Stone, *Holy Baptism*, London, 1912, pp.67-85.

reconcile with a denial of the personal indwelling in those who have been baptized but who have not yet been confirmed'. On the other hand he says that 'in Confirmation the Christian receives a fresh gift of the same divine indwelling to strengthen him for the battle of life'. He goes on to speak of the 'special confirmation gift of the Holy Ghost'. The same teaching is repeated in the Doctrine Report of 1938, as also in the Revised Prayer Book of 1928, which begins by quoting Acts 8 and continues 'The scripture here teaches us that a special gift of the Holy Spirit is bestowed through laying on of hands with prayer'. The same tradition is carried on in *Confirmation Today*.[1] We have noted already that there is a fatal weakness in the doctrine that confirmation is a sacrament of growth, since it cannot be reconciled with infant confirmation. To this the works which we have just quoted have added the further error of tacitly regarding an apostolic origin for confirmation as equivalent to dominical institution.

The attitude of the reformers to confirmation is reproduced succinctly in the report *Christian Initiation: Birth and Growth in the Christian Society* (The Ely Report), which states first that baptism is the full and complete rite of Christian initiation,[2] and later recommends that the rite of confirmation should continue to be administered but only as 'a service of commitment and commissioning'. Dr. Lampe's book *The Seal of the Spirit* supports this view.[3]

Since these three approaches to confirmation are mutually contradictory, it was not unnatural that the authors of some of these reports should look for ways to harmonise the contradictions. All of the official reports with the exception of the Ely report assume without argument that confirmation is a part of initiation. Some of them go on to claim that the Holy Spirit is conveyed both in baptism and confirmation. Thus the Lambeth report of 1948 poses[4] the question 'What is the relation of the gift of the Spirit in baptism to the gift of the Spirit in confirmation?' and goes on to say that 'We are agreed that all consideration of the gifts of the Spirit starts from the recognition of Him as the giver'; but these two quotations are inconsistent, and confuse the gifts which the Spirit gives with the gift of the Spirit. The same confusion appears again in *Baptism and Confirmation Today* (Majority Report), which speaks[5] of 'the gift or gifts of the Spirit' as though they were the same thing. Both of these reports affirm that 'the dissociation of the Holy Spirit from any part of initiation is strongly to be deprecated'. The assumption that confirmation is a true part of initiation is a matter to which we shall turn later. But here we must note the implications of the statements which we have quoted. They are saying either that the gift of the indwelling Spirit may be conveyed partly at baptism and partly at confirmation, which is a denial of Cyprian's dictum that 'the Spirit is not given by measure'; or they are saying that some gifts of the Spirit are given in baptism and others in confirmation, a proposition which omits all

[1] pp.10f.
[2] p.48.
[3] pp.306f.
[4] p.110, Pt. 2.
[5] p.35.

reference to the most important consideration which is the gift of the indwelling Spirit. And both ideas involve the absurd notion that the gift or the gifts of the Spirit may be doled out in two instalments which may be only separated by a matter of ten minutes.

Another proposal[1] designed to resolve the contradictions of the different approaches to confirmation is that the laying on of hands should follow baptism immediately, as it did in the third century, and that it should be performed by the priest. In such circumstances it is supposed that no theological problems would arise, since all the gifts which are conveyed in initiation would be conveyed at one occasion and there would be no need to enquire too closely about which part of the total rite conveyed which gifts. The proposal is presumably based on the assumption that the prayers in the whole rite, and especially the form which accompanied the laying on of hands would be so ambiguously drafted that no clear meaning could be discerned in them. To this we may reply first that such a procedure would solve no problems but only sweep them under the carpet: and that it is a pity to resort to ambiguity unless it is really necessary. Moreover when in the third century baptism was followed immediately by confirmation theological problems did in fact arise almost immediately and Tertullian, as we have seen, had something to say about what was conveyed in baptism and what in confirmation.

[1] e.g. *Report of Lambeth Conference,* 1968, p.99.

4 CONFIRMATION IN THE NEW TESTAMENT

Our enquiry so far has revealed that at least from the end of the second century the western Church has observed a post-baptismal rite which we have come to call confirmation, and we have noted the differences of opinion which exist about its meaning. The question of dominical institution is of critical importance in the debate, for we shall probably agree with St. Thomas Aquinas when he said that to institute a new sacrament belongs to Christ alone. If indeed we can be satisfied that confirmation can be traced either to the command or the example of our Lord, then we should have no reason to doubt that it is an efficacious sacrament. But if we believe that it originated with the apostles only, or possibly that it has some quite different origin, then we should have no reason to regard it as an efficacious sacrament, although we should still be free to think that it might have a useful place in the Church's liturgy, as a subsidiary rite illuminating baptism or as an occasion of commitment and commissioning. To resolve the problem we must turn first to the New Testament.

Two things are clear. One is that in St. Paul's letters there is no certain reference to any post-baptismal rites: but against this it must be added that St. Paul's many references to baptism do not provide certain evidence about any liturgical practices, whether before, during, or after baptism, and that his concern was for the meaning of baptism and not its liturgical details. The other clear fact is that the gospels do not record any command of our Lord which might be taken as the institution of confirmation. Nevertheless, to quote the words[1] of Canon Couratin 'the critical scholar nowadays would probably base the sacraments, not upon Christ's command, but rather upon his example', and some scholars[2] have accordingly detected in the New Testament a thread of duality suggesting a two-stage rite in initiation: and this thread of duality has led them back to our Lord himself, to his example if not his command. The first text which we need to note is St. Peter's address at Pentecost and the words 'Repent and be baptized . . . and you shall receive the gift of the Holy Spirit' (Acts 2.38). This can be taken to mean that the gift of the Holy Spirit is conveyed in baptism. But it is at least possible that St. Peter had in mind not one sacramental action but two, first the baptism and then the gift of the Spirit conveyed in some other rite after baptism. There are not a few passages in the New Testament for which this kind of interpretation has been claimed. Thus we may quote 'Because you are sons, God has sent the Spirit of his Son into your hearts' (Gal. 4.6). We are made sons of God in Baptism: but this text can be interpreted as meaning that we cannot receive the Spirit unless we have first been made sons, and therefore that the gift of the Spirit follows baptism but does not accompany it. In our reading of the Fathers it is always necessary to be careful about their use of the word 'baptism'. There is no doubt that they often use it when what they mean is not only the baptism in water but also the laying on of hands, the anointing, and any

---

[1] *Pelican Guide to Modern Theology,* ed. ed. R. P. C. Hanson, vol. 2, p.137.
[2] e.g. Mason, *op. cit.:* L. S. Thornton, *Confirmation, Its Place in the Baptismal Mystery,* London, 1954: *Baptism and Confirmation Today* (minority report).

other rites and ceremonies which may have been associated with it. We do the same thing ourselves. When we say that a child has been baptized, we do not trouble to add that the godparents made certain promises or that the child was signed with the cross. We take these things for granted and the one word 'baptism' covers them all. In just the same way we must allow for the possibility that when St. Paul or any other New Testament writer speaks of baptism, he *may* have in mind a complex of liturgical action rather than the simple washing in water.

It is possible also to find duality in the narratives of our Lord's baptism. According to St. Luke's account the descent of the Spirit did not accompany the baptism, it followed it. 'When Jesus also had been baptized and was praying, the heaven was opened and the Holy Spirit descended upon him' (Luke 3.21). Accordingly it was not uncommon in the western Church to find in our Lord's baptism a warrant for the prevailing custom of baptizing first and then anointing the candidate, or laying hands on him to convey the Spirit. On the other hand the eastern Church regarded our Lord's baptism as a single event which received its unity from the presence of the Three Persons of the Trinity, the Son in the water, the Father speaking from heaven, and the Spirit descending.

The thread of duality is picked up again in the two occasions when our Lord imparted the Spirit to the apostles, first on Easter Day when 'he breathed on them and said to them "Receive the Holy Spirit" ' (John 20.22), and later at Pentecost in the upper room (Acts 2.1f). Of these two occasions Mason says[1] 'It is natural to suppose that the Paschal gift stands related to the Pentecostal as baptism is related to confirmation.'

The duality which is thus traced from our Lord's baptism to the apostolic teaching and preaching may seem very suggestive. But as evidence for a two-stage rite of initiation instituted by our Lord it is the merest speculation unless it can be supported by evidence that the apostles actually did, as a normal practice, lay hands on people after their baptism, or anoint them after their baptism. The first epistle of St. John is sometimes quoted as evidence of anointing in the apostolic Church to convey the Spirit. He says 'But you have been anointed by the Holy One', and later 'the anointing which you have received from him abides in you, and you have no need that anyone should teach you' (1 John 2.20, 27). It is very probable that when St. John said that his hearers had been anointed he meant that they had received the Holy Spirit. Similarly St. Peter meant that Jesus had received the Holy Spirit when he said 'God anointed Jesus of Nazareth with the Holy Spirit and with power' (Acts 10.30). But St. Peter did not mean that Jesus had literally been anointed. He was using the language of metaphor, and there was no reason to suppose that St. John was doing anything else. The same may just as well be true of St. Paul's words when he said 'Now he which stablisheth us with you in Christ, and hath anointed us, is God' (2 Cor. 1.22). This is another passage which is capable of the interpretation that it refers first to baptism (stablishes us in Christ) and then to confirmation (hath anointed us). However this may be, there is no grounds for certainty that St. Paul meant to be taken literally when he spoke here of anointing.

1 Mason, *op. cit.* p.17.

There remain three important passages which have been taken to indicate that as a regular practice the apostles laid hands on the newly baptized, and that the purpose of this was to convey the Holy Spirit. There is first the account of the baptism of the Samaritans by the deacon Philip, after which the apostles Peter and John 'came down and prayed for them that they might receive the Holy Spirit; for it had not yet fallen on any of them, but they had only been baptized in the name of the Lord Jesus. Then they laid their hands on them and they received the Holy Spirit' (Acts 8.15-17). Similarly there is the narrative about the disciples at Ephesus who had only received the baptism of John. When St. Paul had explained to them the necessity of Christian baptism, the story continues, 'On hearing this they were baptized in the name of the Lord Jesus. And when Paul laid hands on them, the Holy Spirit came on them' (Acts 19.5, 6). These two passages seem to give concrete expression to the duality and to the two stages in Christian initiation at which other passages in the New Testament seemed to hint. In each case baptism is followed by the laying on of hands, and in each case the gift of the Holy Spirit is associated with the laying on of hands to the exclusion of the baptism which preceded it. To these passages we should add a third, from the epistle to the Hebrews, in which the writer of the epistle enumerates 'the doctrines of baptisms and of laying on of hands' among the 'principles of the doctrine of Christ' (Heb. 6.1f). The plural word 'baptisms' is probably accounted for by the fact that a well-instructed Christian would need to know the difference between Christian baptism and the baptism of John, not to mention the lustrations customary among the Jews and the Jewish sects. So here we have a passage in which the laying on of hands is set in immediate association with baptism, and it is difficult to avoid the conclusion that on some occasions at least, though not necessarily always, the laying on of hands after baptism was the practice of the apostolic Church.

It is by no means certain just how much these passages prove. Some have assumed that the practice of the apostles must have been in obedience to the Lord's command or example, and therefore that these passages are sufficient by themselves to prove dominical institution: but this cannot be more than an assumption, and St. Luke gives us no reason to think that it is right. A less confident conclusion from the evidence is reached by E. J. Bicknell. He says 'It is doubtful whether either unction or the laying on of hands can claim any higher authority than that of the custom of the Church. Many hold that the universal use of the laying on of hands by the apostles from the first points back to a definite command of Christ, but that the command has not been preserved. In Hebrews 6.2 the "laying on of hands" is included among the "first principles of Christ".[1] Very possibly this implies that He himself taught it. The arguments are strong but not absolutely conclusive'. Dr. Lampe acknowledges[2] that the text from Hebrews is sufficient to indicate that the laying on of hands after baptism was practiced in the apostolic Church, but not necessarily as the invariable custom. In common with Dom Gregory Dix[3] and Bishop Rawlinson[4] he maintains that

---

[1] E. J. Bicknell, *The Thirty-nine Articles*, (3rd edition, revised by H. J. Carpenter, p.379).
[2] Lampe, *op. cit.* p.79.
[3] G. Dix, *Confirmation, or the Laying on of Hands*, (Theology Occas. Papers, No. 5), p.18.
[4] A. E. J. Rawlinson, *Christian Initiation*, London, 1947, pp.14f.

the passages in the Acts ought not to be accepted as instances of confirmation but of something different. Dix explained them by saying that they are accounts of the ordination of prophets, by which the Holy Spirit endowed the Ephesian disciples, and probably also the Samaritans, with the prophetic power of speaking in tongues. Certainly that was the immediate consequence of the gift of the Spirit to the Ephesian disciples, and very possibly in the case of the Samaritans for the result was apparent to Simon Magus (Acts 8.18). Rawlinson was impressed by the total absence in St. Paul's epistles of any clear reference to the laying on of hands, and claims that in the early days of the Church there was likely to be some diversity of practice, so that customs which were observed in some places by some people were not observed in other places by other people. He then sets out his belief that 'the laying on of hands was in not infrequent use in association with baptism: that as so used it was regarded as a special means whereby the descent of the Spirit on the baptized might be invoked: that there were traditions of its having been attended on particular occasions by outbursts of glossolalia and prophecy: but that it was by no means invariable, nor was it held that the bestowal of the gift of the Spirit on the baptized was so essentially bound up with it as to be contingent on its use'. Dr. Lampe propounds the view that St. Luke's narrative betrays his particular interest in the mission of the Church, that the admission of the Samaritans and Ephesian converts were notable turning points in this mission, and that the laying on of hands which he describes were not cases of confirmation but 'a commissioning for active service in the missionary enterprise'.[1]

Different though the theories of Dix, Rawlinson, and Lampe may be, and although none of them can be any more than theories, they are all agreed in rejecting the common assumption that St. Luke's narratives are designed to provide examples of the normal custom of the Church. It is important to notice that St. Luke nowhere says that they were the normal custom, or even suggests it. We are perfectly entitled to the view that he describes these incidents in Samaria and Ephesus, not because they were the normal thing, but precisely because they were exceptional and therefore demanded to be recorded. Moreover, if St. Luke's purpose was to provide a typical case to show that the laying on of hands normally followed baptism, we may wonder why he does not make his point more clear and why he does not mention the matter in his first account of baptism in the second chapter of Acts.

Taken by themselves, the two passages in Acts and the text in the epistle to the Hebrews have been sufficient to convince some scholars that the laying on of hands after baptism was not unknown in the early Church but that they do not provide the evidence that the practice was universal or 'ordained of Christ'. But if they are taken in conjunction with the accounts of our Lord's baptism, with the two occasions when he imparted the Spirit to the apostles, and with the numerous passages in St. Paul's epistles and elsewhere in which a reference to baptism is followed by mention of the Holy Spirit, it might well seem that we have here a thread of consistent witness to the belief that the Holy Spirit is bestowed not in baptism itself

1 Lampe, *op. cit.* p.78.

but in some other rite which follows it. If this is correct, and we can trace a two-stage rite back from the apostles to an origin in the experience of our Lord in his own baptism and to his action in twice imparting the Holy Spirit to the apostles, then there is a sense in which it might be claimed that confirmation is 'ordained of Christ', on the ground that it originated in his experience and his example, if not in any spoken word. Such is the theory of dominical institution at which Mason seems to hint. We must judge for ourselves whether it sufficiently accounts for the failure of St. Paul to refer anywhere to the laying on of hands: whether the links in the chain of evidence are strong enough to bear the weight which is put upon them: and whether the whole argument is not too speculative to compel our assent in a matter of such importance. Moreover any theory of dominical institution loses in value when it appears that it is not the only theory but one among competing theories, of which there are many.[1] Thus St. Thomas Aquinas stated that our Lord instituted confirmation 'not by conferring it (*exhibendo*) but by promising it'. This view was based on the assurances in the New Testament that our Lord would send the Holy Spirit to the apostles. Burckhard Neunheuser[2] refers us to the Judaic practice of laying on of hands, and continues 'In addition there was the example of the Lord, reaching out his hands as he ascended into heaven, to which we must in all likelihood add a direct dominical command, similar to that given to Ananias': Neunheuser seems to be clutching at straws. One writer of the middles ages claimed that our Lord instituted confirmation when he laid hands on the little children (Mark 10.16): and in recent times Fr. Thornton has given colour to this argument, pointing out that St. Luke, in his account of the same incident (Luke 18.15-17), does not mention the laying on of hands, but that he makes up for the omission in the narratives we have been discussing in Acts.[3] But Thornton does not explain why either of these writers should thus clothe the origins of confirmation in such resolute obscurity.

If the arguments to show that our Lord instituted confirmation fail to convince us, either because of their intrinsic inadequacy or because of their very variety, then we may ask from what source confirmation did arise. In the third century Cyprian of Carthage was the first of many to assume that it originated in the practice of the apostles. It was a natural assumption for him to make. It was the custom of his Church, and when he read the New Testament he observed that the apostles appeared to have the same custom. It would therefore seem reasonable to infer that what happened in his own day was a continuance of what happened in the apostles' day. But it was not necessarily correct, and Fr. Crichton sums up the conclusions of many scholars when he says 'Confirmation does not appear as an identifiable rite until the beginning of the third century, and whatever may be the meaning of Acts 8.15-17 and 19.5ff, these texts seem to have played no part in establishing confirmation in the first three centuries'.[4] There is in fact an interval of a hundred years or more between the date of the last

---

[1] See Fisher, *Christian Initiation: Baptism in the Medieval West*, pp.131f.
[2] B. Neunheuser, *Baptism and Confirmation*, London, 1964, p.48.
[3] Thornton, *op. cit.* p.78.
[4] J. D. Crichton, *Christian Celebration: the Sacraments*, London, 1973, p.88.

book to be written in the New Testament and the first certain evidence for confirmation in Tertullian's treatise *Concerning baptism.* During that hundred years, or even before it in apostolic times, it is possible that an anointing or laying on of hands developed as a subsidiary rite in baptism and many suggestions have been made to show how it might have happened. Anointing, for instance, might have entered the customs of initiation from the ablutionary practices[1] of the ancient world, when they used oil and chrism at the bath where we today use soap and other toiletries. In such circumstances it would have been very natural to see the oil as a symbol of the Holy Spirit, since it was a symbol of the Spirit in Jewish thought. Another possibility is that since Christian baptism might not have seemed much different from John's baptism in its outward appearance, it could have been found desirable to mark the distinction by adding some other rite.[2] It is possible also that both anointing and the laying on of hands might have been imported into Christian initiation customs from the initiation rites of the semi-Christian Gnostic religions.[3] All this is not more than speculation, but it is no more speculative than the assumption that we must trace the origin of confirmation to the events described in the Acts. And in either case, whether confirmation originated in the customs of the apostles or if its origin was even more adventitious, it could only be regarded as a subsidiary rite. It could thus be compared with the sign of the cross in the Anglican baptismal orders. The sign of the cross is not an essential or necessary part of the sacrament, but it is useful in so far as it serves to illuminate the meaning of baptism itself. Similarly the laying on of hands or anointing may serve to illuminate the truth that the Holy Spirit is given in baptism. Such a conclusion is not confined to Anglican scholars. Fr. Crichton writes of confirmation in its relation to baptism in the following terms; 'My own view, for what it is worth, is that in the New Testament all the effects of baptism and confirmation were concentrated in the former sacrament and confirmation, as subsequent centuries have come to know it, is an unfolding of the content of baptism'.[4] Similarly Fr. Yarnold S.J. writes: 'Theologians have had to explain how confirmation confers the Holy Spirit, who has already been conferred in baptism. My own view, for what it is worth, is that confirmation is simply an explicitation of a grace already conferred in baptism'.[5]

---

1 See F. Gavin, *The Jewish Antecedents of the Christian Sacraments,* London, 1928, p.57. also L. L. Mitchell, *Baptismal Anointing,* Alcuin Club, 1966, pp.25f.

2 F. J. Leenhardt, *Le Baptême chrétien,* Neuchatel-Paris, 1944, p.38.

3 Lampe, *op. cit.* pp.120-130.

4 Crichton, *op. cit.* p.104.

5 E. Yarnold, S.J., *The Awe-inspiring Rites of Initiation,* London, 1971, p.31.

5 SYMBOLS OF THE SPIRIT

We may question, however, whether there is any need for a subsidiary rite to illuminate the truth that the Holy Spirit is conveyed in baptism. In the ancient world oil and chrism were commonly recognised as symbols of the Spirit, and the laying on of hands was associated with the conveyance of gifts of all kinds. In the world today, oil is known chiefly as a lubricant and is associated with machinery. If we today were to adopt the use of oil into our liturgical rites, it would need a great deal of explaining if we wished it to be understood. But if a symbol is to be a useful and meaningful sign of what it symbolises, it must carry its meaning on the surface: symbols which need to be explained are dead and outworn symbols,[1] and it would therefore be a mistake to make use of it in the initiation rites today. It would also be quite unnecessary, since water itself was recognised in the ancient world as a symbol of the Holy Spirit, and may still be recognised as such today. Isaiah compared the refreshing power of water and of the Holy Spirit in several passages, notably, 'I will pour water on the thirsty land, and streams on the dry ground: I will pour my Spirit on your descendants' (Is. 44.3), and again 'Until the Spirit is poured upon us from on high and the wilderness becomes a fruitful field' (Is. 32.15). In the light of these passages we should probably be right in supposing that when Joel spoke of the 'outpouring' of the Spirit (Joel 2.28) the image he had in mind was rain pouring from heaven. In St. John's gospel, when Jesus spoke of 'rivers of living water' flowing from the heart of those who believe in him, St. John commented 'This he said about the Spirit, which those who believed in him were to receive' (John 7.38f). St. Paul also speaks of the water of baptism as the place where the Spirit is conveyed to the Christian as a drink (1 Cor. 12.13). The tradition which linked water and the Spirit continued in the Church, both in east and west. Examples of this are not so common in the Fathers of the western Church, although we may mention Irenaeus (*Adversus Haereses* 3.17, 2, 3) and Hilary of Poitiers who said that the Holy Ghost is called 'The River' (*Tract. in Psalm* lxiv.15). It is probable that their interest in chrism as a means of the communication of the Spirit distracted the attention of the western Fathers from the symbolism of water. Nevertheless even as late as the fourth and fifth centuries we find in the catacombs and in other examples of Christian art that scenes of Christian baptism are sometimes depicted showing the dove of the Spirit hovering over the candidate and streams of water flowing over the candidate from the beak of the dove.[2] Nothing could indicate more clearly than this the belief that the gift of the Spirit is associated with the water of baptism. Today, the refreshing quality of water is as well known and as readily appreciated, even in our own more temperate climate, as it was anciently in Palestine, and we have therefore no need to import into our initiation rites additional symbols of the Holy Spirit which are as foreign to our understanding as they are to our ways.

[1] See Crichton, *op. cit.* p.22.

[2] See *Studia Biblica et Ecclesiastica*, vol. 5: C. F. Rogers, *Baptism and Christian Archaeology*. Also F. van der Meer and C. Mohrmann, *Atlas of the Early Christian World*, pp.126f.

6 CONFIRMATION IN THE CHURCHES OF THE EAST

The practice of the eastern Church where confirmation is concerned was originally so far different from the practice of the west that any study of confirmation ignoring the early eastern rite is seriously deficient. Today the custom of the Orthodox Church[1] is not essentially different from that of the west. Infants are baptized and then anointed with chrism, first on the forehead and then on various parts of the body. The words which accompany this anointing are 'The seal of the gift of the Holy Spirit', and this formulary can be traced back at least as far as the year 790, and is probably much older than that. The teaching of the Orthodox Church is that this anointing after baptism conveys the Holy Spirit. This practice and teaching has a long history in the east, and is first attested in the *Catecheses*[2] which were written either by St. Cyril, bishop of Jerusalem from 349 to 386, or by his successor. It has however been convincingly argued by Professor Ratcliff[3] that the post-baptismal anointing was an innovation in the eastern rite which was imported into it in the late fourth century most probably, as Dr. Cuming suggests,[4] from Egypt. Before then the rite of initiation as it was observed in the eastern Church consisted of an anointing *before* baptism followed by the baptism itself. Between the baptism in water and the celebration of the Eucharist which often followed there was no intervening rite, either of anointing or of laying on of hands or anything else. On that point scholars are generally agreed. The anointing was given on the forehead first and then over the whole body. This latter was so thorough that deaconesses were needed at the baptism of women. Then during the moment of baptism, as the candidate stood or kneeled in the water, the priest laid his hand on the candidate's head and baptized him saying 'N., I baptize you in the name, etc.', or at a later date 'N. is baptized in the name, etc.'. And that was all.

Our earliest evidence for a rite of this kind is the *Testaments of the Twelve Patriarchs,*[5] which include the following passage:

4. The first anointed me with holy oil, and gave to me the staff of judgment.

5. The second washed me with pure water and fed me with bread and wine, even the most holy things, and clad me with a holy and glorious robe. (Levi, viii, 4, 5).

M. de Jonge, the most recent editor of this work, agrees with T. W. Manson[6] that this is a description of Christian baptism, and believes that

<hr>

1 *Confirmation, or The Laying on of Hands,* by various writers, vol. 1 (1926), p.281.

2 DBL pp.29f.

3 E. C. Ratcliff, article: 'The Old Syrian Baptismal Tradition', (*Studies in Church History,* ed. G. J. Cuming, 1965, vol. 2), p.32.
See also Dom B. Botte, article: Le Baptême dans l'Eglise syrienne, (*L'Orient syrien,* vol. 1, 1956), p.147: and L. L. Mitchell, *op. cit.* p.48.

4 G. J. Cuming, Article, 'Egyptian Elements in the Jerusalem Liturgy' (*Journal of Theological Studies,* n.s. vol. 25 ,1974).

5 English translation and notes in *Testaments of the Twelve Patriarchs,* ed. R. H. Charles, London, 1908. Notes in *Testaments of the Twelve Patriarchs,* M. de Jonge, Assen, 1953.

6 T. W. Manson, article *Miscellanea Apocalyptica* iii, (*Journal of Theological Studies,* vol. 48).

the *Testaments* were written between the years 190 and 225. The *Didache* was most probably written well before that, and the initiation rite of the *Didache* consists of nothing more than baptism in water in the name of the Trinity.[1] There is no mention of any act of anointing, either before baptism or after it. Dix[2] claimed that no anointing is mentioned in the *Didache* because it was a manual for the laity and not for bishops: but this is to ignore the fact that the unvarying practice of the eastern Church has been that the minister who baptizes the candidate also anoints him. Many documents of the third and fourth centuries[3] attest the old Syrian rite of initiation such as we have described, and although the new form of the rite with the addition of an anointing after baptism is attested from the middle of the fourth century, the old rite without it persisted for a considerable time in some places. Thus Proclus, patriarch of Constantinople from 426 to 446, was evidently not acquainted[4] with the post-baptismal unction: and no more was Narsai, whose homilies on baptism[5] were written in east Syria perhaps half a century later. It is uncertain whether Theodore,[6] bishop of Mopsuestia near Antioch from 392 to 428, attests an anointing after baptism or only a signing with the cross, and uncertain what meaning he attaches to the action, whatever it was. But it seems most probable that he understood it as a sign to show that the candidate had already received the Holy Spirit in his baptism. The Nestorian rite[7] developed from the early rite of Syria, and to this day the Nestorian rite has no ceremony of anointing or of the imposition of the hand after baptism. It provides only that the newly baptized person is signed with the cross, with the words 'N. has been baptized and confirmed (perfected) in the name of the Father, etc.': so this ceremony appears only to look back to the baptism itself and explain it. The Armenian rite[8] was another offshoot from the early rite of Syria. This includes a post-baptismal anointing: but T. Thompson is probably correct in his opinion[9] that the purpose of this anointing is not to convey the Holy Spirit, since there are plain statements in the baptismal formula and elsewhere that this is effected in baptism. The important fact which emerges from the foregoing recital is that a post-baptismal ceremony for the communication of the Spirit was unknown in the Syrian Church until the middle of the fourth century, and was only adopted by slow degrees when it was introduced. Before then, the rite consisted of an anointing before baptism followed only by the baptism itself. The only document which might seem to contradict this account of

---

[1] DBL. p.1. On the strength of the fifth century Coptic ms. of the Didache, J. Daniélou has claimed that the Didache attests a rite of anointing at baptism (*The Christian Centuries*, vol. I, ed. Daniélou and Marrou, London, 1964: p.70): on the other hand Altaner quotes good reason to show that this is a misunderstanding of the coptic text (B. Altaner, *Patrology*, London, 1959: p.52f).

[2] G. Dix, article, 'The Seal in the Second Century' (*Theology*, 1948).

[3] DBL pp.12-50.

[4] A. Wenger, *Huit Catéchèses baptismales*, pp.100f (*Sources chrétiennes*, vol. 50).

[5] DBL pp.50f.

[6] The most convenient translation of Theodore's sermons is in E. Yarnold's *The Awe-inspiring Rites of Initiation*.

[7] H. Denzinger, *Ritus Orientalium*, vol. 1, p.364.

[8] DBL p.60.

[9] T. Thompson, *The Offices of Baptism and Confirmation*, Cambridge, 1914, p.85.

the early Syrian rite is the *Gospel of Philip*.[1] This Gnostic work appears to have originated in Syria in about the middle of the second century. It attests a rite of initiation which consists first of baptism in water, followed by an anointing with chrism, and is then completed in a eucharist. But the *Gospel of Philip* is a bizarre document which owes more to Gnostic speculation than to the Christian faith, and thus differs from many other works which show traces of gnosticism but are nevertheless useful as evidence for Christian practice. Moreover it claims that the sacrament of the chrism is of much greater importance than the sacrament of the water, and on such premises it would be absurd for the anointing to precede the baptism. There is therefore no reason to accept the *Gospel of Philip* as evidence for Christian practice, and if it were so accepted it would be extremely difficult to account for the rest of the Syrian evidence from the *Didache* onwards.[2]

An obvious question arises. At what point in this early Syrian rite did the Christians who used it suppose that the Holy Spirit was communicated to the candidate? Many scholars have jumped to the conclusion that, in the words of T. Thompson, 'the pre-baptismal unction is really the unction of confirmation',[3] and there are passages in the Syrian writers which suggest that this might be so. Thus Narsai says 'It is the Spirit which gives power to the unction of the feeble oil', and also 'the oil receives its power from the Holy Spirit'. But a further examination of his homilies reveals that according to Narsai the effect of the oil is not to communicate the Spirit but to drive away the devil, and to heal the soul. This is unrelated to 'Confirmation'. Moreover in another passage Narsai attributes the gift of the Spirit to the water. He says that the priest 'lays on the drug of the Spirit with the symbol of water'. St. Ephrem Syrus displayed the same inconsistency. In the seventh of his Hymns on Virginity he wrote 'The oil is the agent of the Holy Spirit', which led L. L. Mitchell to comment,[4] rather inaccurately, 'Most evidently the oil is the vehicle of the Holy Spirit'. But this quotation from St. Ephrem needs to be set beside others, such as for instance[5] 'Descend, my brethren, put on from the water of baptism the Holy Spirit'. The *Acts of Thomas*[6] have also been quoted in this connection. These apocryphal stories of occasions when St. Thomas administered baptism attest the Syrian rite of baptism and include prayers for the consecration of the oil. One of these prayers includes the petition 'Come, Holy Spirit, and cleanse their reins and heart', which helped to persuade Professor Ratcliff[7] that the effect of the oil is to convey the Holy Spirit. But this passage must be compared with others which suggest that the oil has the same therapeutic and

1 *The Gospel of Philip*, ed. R. McL. Wilson, London, 1962.

2 Moreover, although E. Segelberg has shown that the *Gospel of Philip* has much to connect it with Antioch (see his article, 'The Antiochene Background to the Gospel of Philip', in *Bulletin de la Société d'Archéologie copte* (Cairo) vol. 18, 1965-66), the Valentinian system of gnosticism which it reflects originated in Alexandria: and the orthodox rites of Alexandria were originally western in character.

3 *op. cit.* p.31.

4 L. L. Mitchell, *op. cit.* p.35. See also Dom. E. Beck, article, 'Le Baptême chez St. Ephrem, (*L.'Orient syrien*, vol. 1, 1956, p.111-136).

5 Works of Ephraim Syrus, Nicene and Post-Nicene Fathers, vol. 13, p.272.

6 DBL. pp.13f.

7 *op cit.* p.26. For further studies of these texts see DBL. pp.xiii-xxii: and E. C. Whitaker, article, 'Unction in the Syrian Baptismal Rite' (*Church Quarterly Review*, 1961).

apotropaic purpose which we noted in the homilies of Narsai. The *Didascalia,* the *Apostolic Constitutions,* and other works have also been drawn on to support the thesis that the anointing before baptism was understood by the early Syrian Church to convey the gift of the Holy Spirit, in spite of the fact that as with Narsai and St. Ephrem, it is often possible to quote other evidence in the same works to indicate the opposite conclusion. The matter was settled with the publication in 1957 of the *Catecheses* of St. John Chrysostom, whose ministry was performed mostly in Antioch until he was made patriarch of Constantinople in the year 398. In this series of addresses[1] to catechumens preparing for baptism, Chrysostom explains that anointing before baptism prepared the candidate as a bride for the nuptials with Christ, and as an athlete in the struggle against the devil. But he makes no suggestion that the Spirit was conveyed in the anointing.

In the face of such authoritative evidence as that which the *Catecheses* of Chrysostom supplies it is no longer possible to contend that the Holy Spirit is conveyed in the anointing before baptism. Some scholars have therefore turned to the argument that the sign which conveyed the Holy Spirit was the action of the priest laying his hands on the head of the candidate as he baptized him. The most important passages to be studied in this connection are also to be found in the *Catecheses* of Chrysostom, and we need to quote them at some length.

1. After this anointing the priest makes you go down into the sacred waters, burying the old man and at the same time raising up the new, who is renewed in the image of his Creator. It is at this moment, through the words and the hand of the priest, that the Holy Spirit descends upon you.

2. When you come to the sacred initiation, the eyes of the flesh see water; the eyes of faith behold the Spirit. Those eyes see the body being baptized; these see the old man being buried . . . Our bodily eyes see the priest as, from above, he lays his right hand on the head and touches (him who is being baptized); our spiritual eyes see the great High Priest as He stretches forth his invisible hand to touch his head. For at that moment, the one who baptizes is not a man but the only-begotten Son of God.

   And what happened in the case of our Master's body also happens in the case of your own. Although John appeared to be holding His body by the head, it was the divine Word which led His body down into the streams of Jordan and baptized Him. The Master's body was baptized by the Word, and by the voice of His Father from heaven which said 'This is my beloved Son' and by the manifestation of the Holy Spirit which descended on Him. This also happens in the case of your body. The baptism is given in the name of the Father and of the Son and of the Holy Spirit . . .

[1] Greek text in A. Wenger, *op. cit.:* E. T. in *St. John Chrysostom, Baptismal Instructions* (Ancient Christian Writers, vol. 31) ed. P. W. Harkins: for further studies see T. T. Finn, *The Liturgy of Baptism in the Baptismal Instructions of St. John Chrysostom,* Washington, D.C., 1967, and H. B. Green, article, 'The Significance of the Pre-baptismal seal in St John Chrysostom' (*Studia Patristica,* vol. vi (1962) pp.84-90).

For this reason, when the priest is baptizing he does not say 'I baptize so-and-so', but 'So-and-so is baptized in the name of the Father and of the Son and of the Holy Spirit'. In this way he shows that it is not he who baptizes but those whose names have been invoked, the Father, the Son, and the Holy Spirit.

These passages include the statement that 'through the words and hand of the priest the Holy Spirit descends on you', and this has been adduced by Lecuyer[1] and Ysebaert[2] as evidence that 'the imposition of hands has acquired a special meaning as the rite which confers the Holy Spirit'. But this is to ignore the evidence, for Chrysostom identifies not only the hand of the priest with the descent of the Spirit but also his words. By this he meant the baptismal formula, which had the effect of associating the three persons of the Trinity with the act of baptism and with its work. Chrysostom compares Christian baptism with the baptism of Jesus, and his argument is that as Jesus was baptized 'by the Word, by the voice of the Father from heaven, and by the manifestation of the Holy Spirit', so all three Persons are engaged in the baptism of the Christian, and perform their work through the ministry of the priest. Chrysostom also says 'When you come to the sacred initiation, the eyes of the flesh see water, the eyes of faith behold the Spirit'. So he finds the Spirit everywhere at baptism, in the words of the priest, in his hand, and in the water. It is therefore not reasonable in the light of such evidence to claim that the imposition of the hand was a sacrament separate from the baptism itself and conveying its own special gift. It was a natural action when baptism by immersion was practiced. Thus in the Epiphany Hymns of St. Ephrem[3] Jesus is represented as saying to John 'Only lay your hand on me' when he asked to be baptized: to speak of the priest baptizing or laying his hand on the candidate meant the same thing in Syrian custom. The imposition of the hand is commonly mentioned in Syrian accounts of baptism, more commonly than in the west, but the commentators do not normally invest it with any special significance, and many regard it as of so little importance that they do not trouble to mention it.

The earliest manuscripts of the liturgical rite of Antioch[4] are not earlier than the eighth century, and it is impossible to determine the date of the materials which the rite incorporates. It includes an anointing after baptism which is associated with the gift of the Spirit. The pre-baptismal anointing is accompanied by a formula which tends to vary from one manuscript to another, but of which the earliest example is as follows: 'N. is signed with the oil of gladness that he may be worthy of the adoption of rebirth, in the name, etc.'. At first sight these words do not seem to suggest that the gift of the Holy Spirit is conferred in the anointing, but Dr. Brock quotes a passage from the sermons of Theodore which might indicate that he regarded the grace of the Spirit as a pre-requisite of the adoption of rebirth. Against this,

1 J. Lecuyer, article, 'San Juan Crisostomo y la Confirmacion' (Orbis Catholica, Barcelona, 1958) p.385.
2 J. Ysebaert, *Greek Baptismal Terminology*, Nijmegen, 1962, p.315, 378.
3 Works of St. Ephraim Syrus, *op. cit.* p.286.
4 Denzinger, *op. cit.* p.267f. See also important article by Dr S. Brock, 'The Syrian Orthodox Baptismal Rite' (*Journal of Theological Studies*, n.s. vol. 23, 1972).

however, we must set Theodore's own interpretation of the anointing before baptism, which has nothing to say about the Spirit but explains the ceremony as an occasion for marking the lambs of the flock of Christ. However the prayer in the Antiochene rite which precedes the anointing calls for our attention. It ran as follows: Holy Father, who through the (hands of) the holy apostles didst give thy Holy Spirit to those who are (being) baptized, do thou now also, using the shadow of my hands, send thy Holy Spirit upon these who are about to be baptized, so that, being filled with it and with its divine gifts, they may produce fruit thirtyfold and sixtyfold and a hundredfold.' Whether this prayer belongs to an earlier or a later stratum of the rite is not known. It is certainly incoherent. The imposition of the hand in the first part of the prayer is undoubtedly a reference to the imposition of the hand in baptism, and the prayer assumes that the custom goes back to the apostles. We should expect this beginning to lead to a petition relating to the act of baptism. In the second part of the prayer, however, the phrase 'the shadow of my hands' seems to be related to the act of anointing, and is certainly related to candidates for baptism before their baptism. Dr. Brock comments on the prayer in these words: 'From this prayer it would appear quite clearly that the old Antiochene tradition of a pre-baptismal anointing connected with the gift of the Holy Spirit has still been preserved in the Antiochene rite, even after the addition of the post-baptismal anointing'. If it was true that the old Antiochene rite connected the anointing before baptism with the gift of the Holy Spirit, we might think it more than a little odd that St. John Chrysostom was evidently unaware of it: and Theodore too in nearby Mopsuestia. Nevertheless we have already observed that some Syrian writers associated the gift of the Holy Spirit with the anointing before baptism, even if they were inconsistent and attributed the gift of the Spirit also to the baptismal washing. The same inconsistency may explain the liturgical rite, for in the prayer for the blessing of the water we find the petition *'Tibi nunc, Domine, complaceat, ut inhabitet Spiritus tuus ille Sanctus super hosce servos tuos, qui baptizantur'*.

The evidence which we have reviewed makes it impossible to suppose that the early Syrian Church had any firm tradition of a second sign in initiation, whether before baptism or during it or after it. It is true that some witnesses traced a connection between the anointing before baptism and the gift of the Spirit, and others between the imposition of the hand and the gift of the Spirit. But the only thing which is constant in the Syrian tradition about the gift of the Spirit is that it is related to the water of baptism, even if some writers also associated the gift with some of the other actions which surrounded the sacrament. It seems probable that the Syrian tradition was accurately summed up in the following passage[1] from the *Apostolic Constitutions:* 'Thou shalt first anoint the person with holy oil, and afterward baptize him with water, and finally shalt seal him with the chrism; that the anointing with oil may be a participation of the Holy Spirit, and the water a symbol of the death, and the chrism a seal of the covenants. But if there be neither oil nor chrism, the water is sufficient both for the anointing and for the seal, and for the confession of him that is dead.'

[1] DBL p.32.

7. CONCLUSION

This brief survey has revealed many uncertainties but one solid fact, and upon it we may build some firm conclusions. This is the fact that the Syrian Church originally had no rite corresponding to the western rite of confirmation, and that they recognised the water of baptism as the one sign by which the gift of the Spirit was certainly effected. This provides the key to the problem whether the narratives in the Acts of the Apostles which we have discussed describe the regular practice of the Church or whether they are a record of incidents which were exceptional. Whatever may be the origin of the practice of the western Church, we have seen that the laying on of hands by the apostles as described in the Acts had no continuing history in the Syrian Church. Their actions cannot therefore be regarded as normative, because in the event they did not prove to be so.

The Syrian rite has something to tell us also about dominical institution. We would accept that our Lord had instituted a sacrament if the New Testament provided indisputable evidence, either from his words or from his example and actions that he had done so: and in such a case we should naturally expect the institution to be proved by the universal observance of the Church from the beginning. Thus our conviction that baptism was instituted by our Lord rests upon the triple foundation of our Lord's words, his example, and the universal practice of the Church. Where confirmation is concerned, our survey has shown us that there is no clear word of the Lord about it, and we have seen much room for question and debate about certain events which might be interpreted as actions or examples of the Lord. The character of the early initiation rite of Syria makes it very plain that the customs associated with baptism which are the subject of this study, although they had a long history in the west, cannot claim the authority of universal observance, since for four centuries and more they were not observed in a substantial part of early christendom.

POST-SCRIPT

The most recent study[1] of the Catecheses of the Syrian Fathers is written by
H. M. Riley, and is an examination of the teaching about initiation by
Theodore, St. John Chrysostom, and St. Cyril of Jerusalem. Riley makes no
attempt to identify the gift of the Spirit with the anointing *before* baptism.
He claims that the anointing *after* baptism is understood by Theodore, and
even by St. Cyril, as nothing more than a symbol of a gift which had already
been conveyed in the earlier parts of the rite. He also argues, as we have
done above, that it is unreasonable to distinguish, as Lecuyer does,
between baptism and the imposition of the hand in baptism, as two
sacramental actions distinct from each other. In spite of these damaging
admissions he avoids the final admission that these Fathers associated
the gift of the Spirit specifically with the sign of water in baptism by claiming
that in their understanding of the matter the gift is conveyed in the whole
complex of the rite in its entirety rather than in any one of its parts, and that
we are not justified in using their writings to confirm theories of sacramental theology which belong to a more logical and schematic school
tradition. To support this contention he quotes a valuable passage from
G. Kretschmar, who compared the 'straight line' tradition of the western
Church, in which the separate rites of initiation are seen to follow each
other, each in its consecutive order and each with its own peculiar significance, with the 'circular' tradition of the eastern Church, where 'the
capacity grew ever stronger to view the various rites of baptism looking
out from a central point as it were, the baptismal bath, as the unfolding of
the one baptism according to the laws of the divine economy of salvation'.[2]

These arguments only avoid an open admission of the plain truth by
wrapping it in obscurity. It is true that these Fathers did not trouble to
lay down explicit distinctions between essential rites and inessential, and
that they treat apotaxis, syntaxis, anointings wherever they occur, divesting
of clothes and putting them on again, and all the rest, as equal parts of the
received tradition with the baptism itself, and that they often assigned to
inessential parts of the rite a significance which belonged to the essence of
initiation. Nevertheless we are justified in the belief that the gift of the Holy
Spirit, like all the other gifts which are conveyed in initiation, is given by
some sign which is outward and effectual, and which must be essential
to the rite. And if, as Riley correctly tells us, this sign is not either of the
anointings and not the imposition of the hand in baptism, and if, as he
rightly claims, the bath is central and the rest peripheral, then we are driven
to the conclusion that it can only be the sign of the water of baptism in the
name of the Holy Trinity, the sign which stands at the centre to which all
else is ancillary.

[1] *Christian Initiation,* by Hugh M. Riley (Studies in Christian Antiquity, ed. J. Quasten,
    no. 17) Catholic University of America Press, 1974.
[2] G. Kretschmar, *Die Geschichte des Taufgottesdienstes in der alten Kirche,* in Leiturgia,
    Handbuch des evangelischen Gottesdienstes, eds. K. Muller, W. Blankenburg,
    vol. 5, Der Taufgottesdienst (Kassel, 1970) p.236.

GROVE BOOKLETS ON MINISTRY AND WORSHIP

Published one each month—24 (or more) pages. Titles asterisked are in second edition or a reprint. Cost 20p, except where otherwise stated.

Nos. 4 and 11 are out of print and unlikely to be reprinted

Write for Catalogue of other publications

Other Publications on **LITURGY**

GROVE LITURGICAL STUDIES—A quarterly series—32 pages—**55p**

1. **Sacramental Initiation Complete in Baptism** by E. C. Whitaker